National Institute of
Standards and Technology
U.S. Department of Commerce

NISTIR 7617

Mobile Forensic Reference Materials:

A Methodology and Reification

Wayne Jansen
Aurélien Delaitre

NISTIR 7617

Mobile Forensic Reference Materials:
A Methodology and Reification

Wayne Jansen
Aurélien Delaitre

COMPUTER SECURITY

Computer Security Division
Information Technology Laboratory
National Institute of Standards and Technology
Gaithersburg, MD 20899-8930

October 2009

U.S. Department of Commerce
Gary Locke, Secretary

National Institute of Standards and Technology
Patrick D. Gallagher, Deputy Director

Reports on Computer Systems Technology

The Information Technology Laboratory (ITL) at the National Institute of Standards and Technology (NIST) promotes the U.S. economy and public welfare by providing technical leadership for the Nation's measurement and standards infrastructure. ITL develops tests, test methods, reference data, proof of concept implementations, and technical analysis to advance the development and productive use of information technology. ITL's responsibilities include the development of technical, physical, administrative, and management standards and guidelines for the cost-effective security and privacy of sensitive unclassified information in Federal computer systems. This Interagency Report discusses ITL's research, guidance, and outreach efforts in computer security, and its collaborative activities with industry, government, and academic organizations.

National Institute of Standards and Technology Interagency Report
35 pages (2009)

Abstract

This report concerns the theoretical and practical issues with automatically populating mobile devices with reference test data for use as reference materials in validation of forensic tools. It describes an application and data set developed to populate identity modules and highlights subtleties involved in the process. Intriguing results attained by recent versions of commonly-used forensic tools when used to recover the populated data are also discussed. The results indicate that reference materials can be used to identify a variety of inaccuracies that exist in present-day forensic tools.

Keywords: *Mobile Devices, Computer Forensics, Forensic Tool Validation*

iv

Table of Contents

1. Introduction

Forensic specialists today operate within what can be termed the forensic tool spiral, illustrated in Figure 1. New versions of forensic tools are issued regularly by a tool manufacturer to provide new features, broaden the range of existing functions, and correct identified problems. To ensure that a new or updated forensic tool is suitable for use by an organization, it must first be validated. After the organization completes validation of the tool successfully, it can safely be put into use for its intended purpose [SWG09].

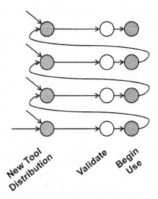

Figure 1: Forensic Tool Validation Spiral

Validation involves populating a sample device with representative test data and confirming successful recovery of the data [Goo03]. Populating a device is time consuming and prone to error, especially if done manually. The situation often creates an impasse —the improvements to the tool would benefit the work being performed, but no convenient time is immediately available to validate the tool. These circumstances could induce individuals to take a risk and use an updated tool without first validating it. The predicament could be alleviated greatly, if validation could be expedited, possibly by devising a means to populate mobile devices readily with reference test data, to create reference material for use in tool assessment. This report explores a general approach and specific implementation for creating reference material along the line suggested.

2. Background

Reference material is commonly used in other scientific areas to control the quality of products. The term generally refers to a substance that is stable with respect to one or more specified properties and has been deemed suited for use in a measurement process [EPS01]. For example, if a device detects a contaminant within a liquid, it would be useful to have sample solutions with different concentrations of the contaminant to determine the accuracy of the device or to calibrate the device. A single reference material, however, should not be used both to calibrate and validate results in the same measurement procedure.

Reference materials can be used for various purposes, including the following:

- To help develop accurate methods of analysis
- To calibrate measurement systems used to institute quality control, determine performance characteristics, or measure a property at the state-of-the-art limit
- To assess measurement procedures and validate methods
- To use in proficiency tests
- To ensure the adequacy and integrity of measurement quality assurance programs.

In general, the need for reference materials is vital in forensic analytical laboratories, where quality assurance is a major issue. It is the premise of the report that reference materials with the needed properties could be produced straightforwardly and used to validate mobile forensic tools, identifying inaccuracies that otherwise might go unnoticed.[1]

---

[1] The reference material described in this report is not to be confused with NIST Standard Reference Materials - http://ts.nist.gov/measurementservices/referencematerials/index.cfm.

3. Forensic Reference Material

For cell phones, the most common type of mobile device, three components are of interest: the handset, the identity module, and the removable memory card. The memory of the handset typically contains the widest range of data, since it is involved with both the cellular interface and the data processing capabilities. Moreover, the structure of the data it contains may be dictated to some extent by the capabilities of the handset. The identity module is more limited in the range of data it contains, although still quite extensive, and related to the cellular interface in part. The structure of the data is also standardized to a high degree. Removable memory cards, while having the broadest range of data, are less of a problem, since they can be treated using traditional forensic procedures similar to those used with disk drives. Therefore, they are not discussed further in this report.

Empirical assessment of algorithms used by forensic tools to recover evidence is predicated on using reference materials (i.e., exemplar devices containing known data). Populating a device with a representative set of data to create reference material can be done in various ways:

- Manually – Using manual means to populate a group of individual items onto a device is typically a time-consuming and error-prone process. Because of that, the test coverage may be restricted to the most essential items to expedite the process.
- Semi-automated – Using a semi-automated process typically preserves manually populated data for reuse. For example, an image from a manually populated handset may be captured and later flashed onto the same handset or model of handset to recreate the reference test material.
- Automated – Using an automated means to populate devices can greatly expedite validation, once the initial effort to construct the test data is completed. For example, a smart card scripting tool can be used to create a script that populates identity modules.

Different types of devices generally require different techniques to populate data. Different techniques can require deeper levels of skill and knowledge and produce varying levels of coverage. In particular, as mentioned above, manual techniques can limit the range of coverage of possible data types. For example, populating an identity module manually might involve resetting the default language of a handset to enable foreign language characters to be populated. Navigation among menu entries needed to create different types of data can be difficult and slow, if the user is not very familiar with the language in question. Ideally, one would like a technique that is automated, simple to use, and comprehensive in coverage.

4. Identity Modules

Identity modules are trusted hardware designed to store and process data and to act as security tokens for gaining access to cellular services. Identity modules are highly standardized, have a straightforward communications interface, and are prevalent in a wide range of cell phones. Forensic tools to recover data from identity modules were also the earliest form of forensic tool for cell phones, and from a maturity perspective should be highly reliable and accurate. In addition, nearly all mobile forensic tools, almost without exception, deal with identity modules either exclusively or as one component of an integrated toolkit. Finally, test data established for identity modules typically apply as well to the handset. Therefore, identity modules present a good starting point for investigating the benefits and drawbacks in creating reference materials for mobile forensics.

The most common identity modules are Subscriber Identity Modules (SIMs) for second generation (2G) GSM phones. Backwards-compatible 2G/3G UMTS SIMs (USIMs) are also supported by the prevailing standards and quite common today [3GPP09c]. Other types of identity modules also exist, including those for iDEN phones and Removable User Identity Modules (R-UIMs) for CDMA phones. The early identity module standards developed for SIMs established the paradigm for content and functionality seen in other identity modules that followed. Moreover, data stores for a SIM also cover a major subset of the data stores of a 3G USIM [3GPP09c]. Hence, they serve well to illustrate the overall principles and nuances involved with populating test data onto identity modules.

4.1   File System Organization

SIMs are specialized smart cards that contain a processor and memory. A file system resides in persistent memory and is hierarchically structured. Three main components are the Master File (MF) or root of the file system, Dedicated Files (DF) that serve as directories, and Elementary Files (EF) that hold data content. Elementary Files can retain data in several forms: as a sequence of bytes that form a record (transparent), a one-dimensional array of records (linear fixed), and a last-in first-out queue of records (cyclic). Figure 2 illustrates the file system hierarchy and forms of EF content.

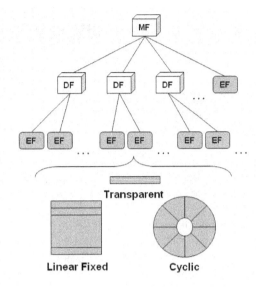

Figure 2: SIM File System

4.2 Data Coverage

While the organization of the file stores is simple, many subtleties exist that affect the range of coverage of test data. They include the extent and idiosyncrasies of character set encodings that are available, and the data structures and relationships that can be exhibited. Gaining write access to the various EFs on a SIM that typically contain data of interest to an examiner is also a related issue affecting test data coverage. These three main areas affecting test coverage are shown in Figure 3.

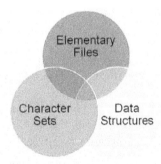

Figure 3: Areas of Test Coverage

Previous work carried out in the assessment of forensic SIM tools identified a variety of shortcomings [Aye05, Aye07, Jan06]. Many of those shortcomings suggest that the tools were vetted by the manufacturers for only a narrow range of commonly encountered data and would benefit from more broadened test coverage.

5. Character Sets

A surprisingly wide range of character sets and encodings exist for populating EFs. In many ways, the encodings used with SIMs and other identity modules hark back to the early days of computing when memory was at a premium and every bit was put to full use. In some cases, the data structures can be quite convoluted, such as in the following example where two integer values are defined, one a 12-bit unsigned integer and the other a 4-bit signed integer [3GPP07]: "Byte 4 and bits b1 to b4 of byte 5 represent the Elementary Price per Unit (EPPU) in the currency coded by bytes 1-3. Bits b5 to b8 of byte 5 are the decimal logarithm of the multiplicative factor represented by the absolute value of its decimal logarithm (EX) and the sign of EX, which is coded 0 for a positive sign and 1 for a negative sign."

Besides variable-length, signed and unsigned integers expressed in binary, numbers can be expressed in Binary Coded Decimal (BCD) [3GPP07]. BCD encodes each decimal digit that makes up a number into 4-bit nibbles, which allows faster conversion for display and entry than does a binary representation of the complete number. Single and short multi-bit fields are also common, used for flag settings, enumerated types, and low-valued integers. The most variation exists in the expression of characters used in message content and in so-called alpha identifiers. Three general types of character encodings are supported: 7-bit GSM, 8-bit representations, and 16-bit UCS2. Each encoding scheme has interesting aspects to it, discussed below.

Ideally, the full range of values for elementary file content would be represented in the reference test data. However, because the available memory is very limited, expressing a full range of possibilities on a single identity module is not practicable. Instead, concentrating on more commonly used encodings and exploring the variability possible within those encodings can be accomplished more readily. Multiple identity modules can also be populated with portions of the reference test data to expand coverage.

5.1   GSM 7-bit Character Set

The GSM standards define a basic, 128-character, default character set that uses a 7-bit encoding [3GPP08]. Support for the 7-bit GSM character set is mandatory. The character set includes the upper and lowercase 26-character English alphabet, the Arabic numerals 0 through 9, numerous special characters, and other characters used in Latin and non-Latin languages. 7-bit characters are normally packed into 8-bit bytes to utilize bits that would other go unused. For example, a 140 byte message when packed affords 160 characters of text.

The GSM standards also specify an extension mechanism for defining additional characters [3GPP08]. A sparsely-populated extension table for symbols of international significance, such as the Euro currency symbol, is included in the standards. To encode a character in the extension table, two septets are required: the first for the escape character in the basic alphabet, the second for the character in the extension table. Besides the Euro symbol, the following special characters (in quotes) are currently defined: "^" "{" "}" "\" "[" "~" "]" "|". If a code for an extension table entry is encountered for which no symbol has been specified, then the corresponding character in the basic GSM 7-bit alphabet should be used.

5.2 UCS2 16-bit Character Set

GSM standards support the 16-bit UCS2 character set standardized by ISO/IEC to allow use of an extensive range of national-specific character sets beyond that of 7-bit GSM [3GPP07]. Three different forms of encoding are defined. The first octet of each encoding indicates the type of encoding: 81, 82, or 83. Type 81 encodings are straight forward, consisting of a sequence of 16-bit UCS2 character codes. Type 82 and 83 encodings are a bit more complicated.

The second octet of a type 82 encoding indicates the number of characters in the string, while the third octet contains an 8-bit number that defines the most significant portion or prefix of a 16-bit base pointer to a character table in the UCS2 code space. The remaining 8-bit codes are used as a suffix to identify a specific UCS2 character or, somewhat surprisingly, a 7-bit GSM character, depending on the setting of the most significant bit (i.e., 0 for GSM, 1 for UCS2 suffix). The second octet of a type 83 encoding indicates the length of the string as before. The third and fourth octets define an entire 16-bit base pointer to a character table. The remaining 8-bit codes are used as an offset from the base pointer to identify a specific UCS2 character or, as above, a 7-bit GSM character.

5.3 8-bit Character Sets

8-bit data can occur in both alpha identifiers and message content. When used in alpha identifiers, such as names in address book entries, the 7-bit GSM encoding is typically used with the additional most significant 8th bit set to zero. When used in message content, it implies that a user-defined coding applies.

7

6. Data Structures

Basic relationships can exist between records in different EFs or within the same EF. A simple example is the relationship between the IMSI and AD EFs. A field in AD conveys the length of MNC in the IMSI, which is needed to interpret the IMSI correctly. More involved relationships also exist, as discussed below.

6.1   Linked Extensions

Various extension EFs in the file system are used to contain overflow information from entries in other EFs and provide a good example of a common data structure. Several EFs are defined for this purpose: EXT1, EXT2, EXT3, and EXT4. For instance, if the number field of an ADN EF entry exceeds 20 digits, the remaining digits can be stored in an EXT1 EF entry, as illustrated in Figure 4 for a 24-digit number with an alpha identifier of "John [home]." A field in the ADN entry contains the index of the EXT1 entry that contains the remaining digits, which in this case is the 2nd entry. That is, the index serves as a physical link to where the overflow information is stored.

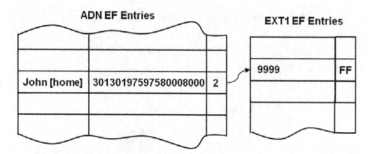

Figure 4: ADN Number Field Overflow Example

Note that longer numbers can also be accommodated. For example, if the second EXT1 entry were insufficient, another available EXT1 entry, say the third entry, could hold the overflow digits and be linked forward from the second EXT1 entry via an index value (i.e., 3), as shown in Figure 5. The index value FF in the third entry indicates that no further links apply. The procedure essentially forms a linked list or chain of EXT1 entries to hold overflow data.

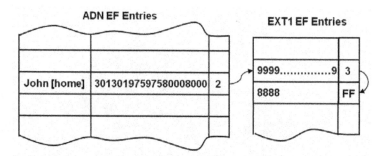

Figure 5: EXT1 Overflow Chain Example

Interestingly, it is possible to encode the EXT1 entries to form a circular list. That is, the FF terminating value could be changed to point to the entry in which it resides or to an entry that links back to it. While this would be considered an abnormal setting, it would be possible for someone to program such a change to poison the content, as an anti-forensic technique to affect processing by a forensic SIM tool.

6.2 Message Segments

Text messages are exchanged between subscribers via one or more short message segments. Each entry in the SMS EF holds one message segment. The maximum allowable length of textual content per segment is 140 bytes per message. Longer messages are split into multiple message segments that can be reassembled [3GPP09a]. Zero length messages that contain no user data and only message header data are also possible.

A message segment has numerous fields that relate to the message type. A message reference field conveys a reference number assigned to the message when submitted by a mobile device. The originating and destination addresses, service center time stamp, and user data length are other important fields, besides the actual user data content. Various flags are also conveyed that indicate the disposition of a message (e.g., whether it is incoming or outgoing, and respectively read or sent).

Segments that make up a concatenated message are linked to each other logically through reference numbers. Every message segment that makes up the concatenated message has the same message reference number. Two other message number fields are used to assemble and control those segments: the segment index and the segment count. The segment index indicates the sequence number of a particular short message within the concatenated message. The value starts at 1 and increases by 1, up to a maximum of 255, for each message segment sent. The segment count indicates the total number of short messages that make up the concatenated message and ranges from 0 to 255. Figure 6 illustrates these messages number fields used in a 3-segment concatenated message whose reference number is 65 and individual segment index/segment count numbers are respectively 1/3, 2/3, and 3/3. Note that the braces in the message body are a convention used in the reference data to provide a visual cue that other segments may follow or precede a given segment.

SMS EF Entries

Figure 6: Concatenated Message Example

9

Message segments that make up a concatenated message are not necessarily stored in consecutive slots of the SMS EF, in contrast to Figure 6. Over time, message deletions tend to fragment the available slots in the EF, somewhat similar to disk fragmentation. It is also possible to have situations where some message segments of a concatenated message are not present. For example, once a message is read and deleted, some segments may be reused and the contents overwritten, while other segments remain and their contents are able to be recovered.

SMS message content can be extended through the Enhanced Messaging Service (EMS) to allow simple multimedia messages to be conveyed. Segments of an EMS message reside in the SMS EF. EMS messages are essentially an application-level content extension to SMS, which conform to the general SMS message structure and support for concatenated messages. The second segment in Figure 7 illustrates an EMS object conveyed as part of a two-segment concatenated message.

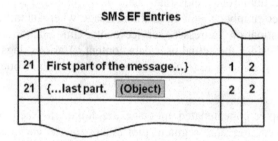

Figure 7: Example EMS Message

EMS messages can contain not only formatted text with different font styles and fonts, but also simple animations, black and white bitmap pictures, monophonic melodies, and vCard and vCalendar objects [3GPP09a]. Several EMS objects may be mixed together in one message and are encoded in the user data portion of a message as information elements within the user data header. The presence of EMS objects significantly increases the complexity of message content and, because of the additional content encoding, EMS messages usually require more than a single message segment.

7.   Elementary Files

An assortment of digital evidence from a SIM lies scattered throughout various EFs in the file system. For a reference SIM to be useful, its file system must be populated with test data that is normally recovered by such tools and of interest to examiners. Several general categories of data apply:

- Service-related Information
- Phonebook and Call Information
- Messaging Information
- Location Information.

Table 1 lists a number of EFs from each of these categories that contain data regularly employed by forensic examiners and useful as core items for validation [Dea05, Wil03].

Table 1: Core Forensic SIM Data

Category	EF	Description
Service-related Information	ICCID	The Integrated Circuit Card Identifier (ICCID) is a unique numeric identifier for the SIM that can be up to 20 digits long. It consists of an identifier prefix (89 for telecommunications), followed by a country code, an issuer identifier number, and an individual account identification number [ITU06]. Aside from the prefix, the components of an ICCID are variable.
	IMSI	The International Mobile Subscriber Identity (IMSI) is a unique 15-digit numeric identifier assigned to the subscriber. Its structure is somewhat similar to the ICCID: a Mobile Country Code (MCC), a Mobile Network Code (MNC), and a Mobile Subscriber Identity Number (MSIN). The MCC is 3 digits, the MNC may be either 2 or 3 digits, and the MSIN assigned by the carrier takes up the remainder. The fourth byte of another EF, Administrative Data (AD), gives the length of the MNC [3GPP09b].
	MSISDN	The Mobile Station International Subscriber Directory Number (MSISDN) is intended to convey the telephone number assigned to the subscriber for receiving calls on the phone, but is updatable by the subscriber. Unlike the ICCID and IMSI, however, the MSISDN is an optional EF.
	SPN	The Service Provider Name (SPN) is an optional EF that contains the name of the service provider. If present, it can be updated only by the administrator (i.e., Administrator access).
	SDN	The Service Dialling Numbers (SDN) is an optional EF that contains numbers for special services such as customer care.
	EXT3	The Extension3 (EXT3) EF contains additional data for SDN entries.
Phonebook and Call Information	ADN	The Abbreviated Dialling Numbers (ADN) EF retains a list of names and phone numbers entered by the subscriber. The type of number (TON) and numbering plan identification (NPI) are also maintained in this EF. It also holds an index to an EXT1 EF record for overflow data (i.e., an unusually long sequence of digits).
	LND	The Last Numbers Dialled (LND) EF contains a list of the most recent phone numbers called by the device. A name may also be associated with an entry (e.g., a called phonebook entry) and stored with the number. It also holds an index to an EXT1 EF record for overflow data.
	EXT1	The Extension1 (EXT1) EF record is used to maintain overflow digits for ADN, LND, and other EF entries.
	FDN	The Fixed Dialling Numbers (FDN) EF is similar to ADN insofar as a list of names

11

Category	EF	Description
		and phone numbers is involved, but restricts dialing to just the numbers prescribed by a card manager. If the FDN storage capacity cannot hold all of the information for an entry, an index to an Extension2 (EXT2) EF record is used to indicate where the additional data is maintained.
	EXT2	The Extension2 (EXT2) EF record is used to maintain overflow digits for FDN and other EF entries.
Messaging Information	SMS	The Short Message Service (SMS) EF contains text and associated parameters for messages received from or sent to the network, or are to be sent out as an MS-originated message. SMS entries contain text and header information such as the time an incoming message was sent as recorded by the mobile phone network, the sender's phone number, the SMS Center address, and the status of the entry. The status of an entry can be designated as unoccupied free space or as occupied by one of the following: a received message to be read, a received message that has been read, an outgoing message to be sent, or an outgoing message that has been sent. Deleted messages are usually flagged as free space and the content left unchanged on the SIM until overwritten.
Location Information	LOCI	The Location Information (LOCI) EF contains the Location Area Information (LAI) for voice communications. The LAI is composed of the MCC and MNC of the location area and the Location Area Code (LAC), an identifier for a collection of cells [3GPP09b].
Location Information	LOCI GPRS	The GPRS Location Information (LOCIGPRS) EF contains the Routing Area Information (RAI) for data communications over the General Packet Radio Service (GPRS). The RAI is composed of the MCC and MNC of the routing area and the LAC, as well as a Routing Area Code (RAC), an identifier of the routing area within the LAC.

To control the conditions of access to elements of the file system, levels of rights are assigned to EFs, DFs, and the MF [3GPP07]. The SIM operating system regulates access to an element of the file system based on the type of action being attempted and the access condition [3GPP07]. The following access conditions can apply:

- Always - Action can be performed without any restriction
- Card Holder Verification 1 (CHV1) - Action can be performed only after a successful verification of the user's PIN, or if PIN verification is disabled
- Card Holder Verification 2 (CHV2) - Action can be performed only after a successful verification of the user's PIN2, or if PIN2 verification is disabled
- Administrative - Action can be performed only after prescribed requirements for administrative access are fulfilled
- Never - Action over the SIM/ME interface is forbidden.

Actions on EFs include searching, reading, and updating the contents. For example, while reading and searching the contents of a particular EF might be allowed without CHV1 verification (i.e., an Always access condition applies), updating might likely require CHV1 being correctly verified (i.e., a CHV1 access condition applies). In general, CHV1 protects core SIM data for the card user against unauthorized reading and updating, while CHV2 protects administrative dialing control data mainly for a card manager (e.g., the administrator of an organizational subscriber), if such a relationship exists. The 4 to 8 digit values of both CHVs can be reset by anyone knowing the PIN values, or their verification completely disabled. So-called ADM Codes are required for Administrative access and are normally kept by the service provider or network operator that issued the SIM.

Reference data can be populated on a SIM only when the correct access conditions are satisfied for performing update (i.e., write) operations. Table 2 identifies the access conditions required to write data to the EFs discussed earlier.[2]

Table 2: Access Conditions for Selected EFs

CHV1	CHV2	ADM	NEVER
ADN	FDN	IMSI	ICCID
EXT1	EXT2	SDN	
LND		EXT3	
SMS		SPN	
LOCI		AD	
LOCIGPRS		PHASE	
MSISDN			

ADM access is normally available only to the issuer of a SIM. This limits the range of data that can be populated. Fortunately, two classes of SIMs are generally available: production SIMs for subscribers and test SIMs for developers. CHV values are usually available for most production SIMs; however, for test SIMs, ADM codes are usually provided together with the CHV values. Production SIMs can still form a useful baseline for validation, but require that EFs unable to be populated are noted and taken into account during tool validation.

---

[2] Note that with some developer identity modules, it is possible to update the ICCID, contrary to its access condition.

8. Layers of Abstraction

Forensic SIM tools, as with other forensic tools, offer various levels of abstraction to the examiner. Figure 8 illustrates the levels involved, starting with the lowest level at the bottom to the highest level at the top, along with two examples of data transformations for the contents of the LAI EF and the LND and EXT1 EFs.

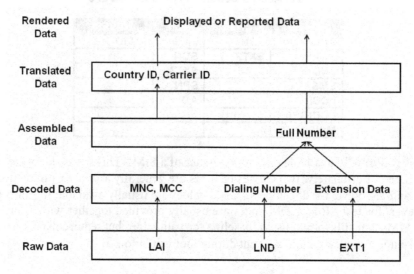

Figure 8: Levels of Abstraction

At level 1, the lowest level, the raw data recovered by the tool is made available, either on a field-by-field basis or as a complete record. While in many cases the data is difficult to interpret, it may nevertheless be provided as a detailed accounting of the tool's activities. At level 2, raw data is decoded to a more human readable form. Decoding of packed 7-bit GSM encoded messages is a good example of this utility. Decoding even more simple data transformations can be of benefit and another example.

At level 3, a tool may go further and assemble together pieces of decoded data for the examiner. For example, message segments that form a concatenated message could be combined to simplify the examiner's task of having to link the together the components to read and understand the complete message. LND entries with numbers that overflow into EXT1 is another area where a level 3 abstraction could apply, by presenting the entire set of digits in the number as a single value. Finally, at level 4, translation from values of lower forms of data to more meaningful information occurs. Two types of translation can occur: that from values into labels or identifiers specified in the governing standard and that from values into labels or identifiers assembled by the tool manufacturer. An example of the former is the translation of the Language Preference (LP) (i.e., a numeric) or the Extended Language Preference (ELP) (i.e., a 2-character abbreviation) EFs into the name of the language (e.g., English, French, and Japanese). An example of the latter is the translation of the MCC and MNC portions of the LAI field of the LOCI EF into a country name and network carrier identifier respectively.

Different forensic tools may provide different layers of abstraction to a user for the same EF content. This can be a source of confusion for a forensic examiner who uses multiple tools; it also complicates the validation process, since data can be legitimately represented in multiple ways. Sometimes data can also be reported at more than one level of abstraction by a forensic tool. In fact, it would be desirable to have a log of all transactions performed by a tool (i.e., level 1 raw data), in addition to data reported at higher levels of abstraction, as a means for ensuring the tool's correct operation.

As might be expected, the more functionality a tool incorporates to provide higher levels of abstraction, the greater the complexity and susceptibility to error. Figure 9 illustrates the general relationship and identifies some common issues involved.

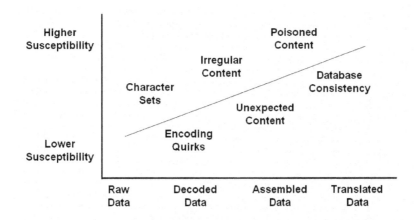

Figure 9: Levels of Abstraction versus Susceptibility to Error

The common issues described below are not necessarily restricted only to forensic SIM tools. They may also apply to tools for the handset and memory card, which may contain identical or similar data.

- Character sets – the wide range of encodings that are possible can give rise to inaccuracies.
- Encoding quirks – lapses in coverage of special cases, such as the two-septet escape codes for 7-bit GSM Extensions and two-character MNCs found in North American IMSIs, can occur.
- Irregular content – Common conventions may not be followed by all carriers, such as T-Mobile not encoding the length of the MNC in the AD EF, creating a need for special treatment to compensate.
- Unexpected content – Content can be correct, such as zero length messages or deleted concatenated messages that have some segments overwritten, but unexpected and handled incorrectly.
- Poisoned content – Since some content is under the subscriber's control, it may be purposefully changed, such as creating a circular list of EXT1 entries, to create problems for a forensic tool.

15

- Database consistency – Any mechanism a tool uses to translate codes into meaningful labels, such as the MNC mappings into network carrier names, needs to be kept up-to-date over time (e.g., when carriers merge or when one carrier buys another).

9. Application Design

Automatically populating an identity module with test data is typically done using an editor tool designed for smart cards or identity modules that includes scripting capabilities. Commands typically follow a simple format with keywords and parameters that the tool understands to perform associated activities, such as locating an EF and writing data to it. The commands are translated into Application Programming Data Units (APDUs) that are sent to the identity module for processing.

Several commands can be linked together in a script and executed, using additional commands to control the flow of execution. For example, if a referenced EF does not exist or a command fails for some other reason, the flow of control needs to be programmed to catch such conditions and debugged, much like a programming language. Gaining expertise with a new command language and preparing scripts is a serious drawback to this approach. Another drawback is that the flexibility offered by a scripting language is low. Typically the data to be populated is embedded within the script, making modification and update more demanding than should be necessary.

The design strategy for populating identity modules advocated in this report is straightforward and largely avoids the problems with preparing editor scripts. The primary principle is that data content is kept separate from device programming. Instead, programming is data driven, guided entirely by the data content made available to it. The data is highly structured, and its syntax must meet the requirements for a well-formed XML document. The data must also conform to the XML schema definitions (i.e., be a valid XML document) defined for the application.

The application contains the control logic, APDU construction, and communications for populating the identity module based on the data elements encountered. Figure 10 illustrates the overall data flow for a desktop application, shown as a circle, to populate SIMs. Two types of XML data files are used by the application: a reference data file and a card file. The reference data file contains the data to be populated onto a single SIM. The card file contains information about the SIM card to be populated, such as the PIN codes needed to access files and other card-specific information. The application also uses the XML schema definition files to which the data and card file content conforms.

17

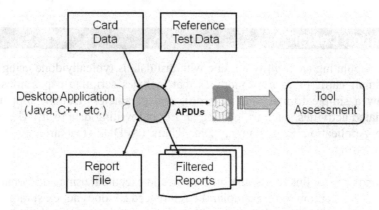

Figure 10: Application Data Flow

As the population procedure progresses, detailed entries are made to the report file, including the APDUs exchanged and success or failure of the operation. The reference data includes some content that may only be able to be populated on certain developer SIMs, since ADM access is needed. Populating SIMs issued by cellular carriers typically results in a failure notification in the report file for those items requiring ADM access and they are not populated. The application has the capability to apply various levels of filtering to entries in the report file to allow one to view the contents at an appropriate level of detail as a filtered report.

The choice of XML for the representation of data brings with it several advantages. XML is a well-known and well-defined standard, similar to HTML, and users are likely to have some familiarity with it. XML schema definitions specified for a document can be used to define its contents and exert control at a low level of detail. Schema-sensitive XML editors are widely available, and many of them are free. These editors make it fairly easy to modify existing or create new reference test data conforming to the schema definition, once some familiarity is gained with the data elements.

18

10.   Reference Test Data

The reference test data set used as a baseline to populate SIMs was assembled manually, building on studies carried out previously [Aye05, Aye07]. The XML-structured data also lends itself to automatic generation of test data to compose more aggressive tests. For example, fuzzing, a type of fault injection technique that involves sending various types of pseudorandom data to available interfaces to discover unknown flaws, could be used [Jur06]. However, the intent was to provide a more realistic representation of content that can be composed by cellular subscribers when using existing handsets and by cellular operators when issuing SIMs.

The resulting set of reference data comprises three XML files, each containing data to populate a single SIM. They are, for lack of imagination, referred to as SIM1, SIM2, and SIM3. The SIM1.xml and SIM2.xml files contain basic reference data cases, while SIM3.xml contains unconventional data cases under consideration and used primarily for experimentation. Figure 11 illustrates the situation.

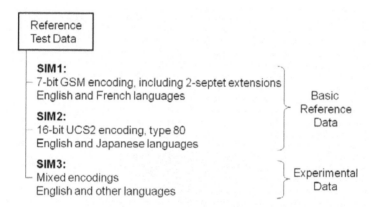

Figure 11: XML Reference Data Files

SIM1 and SIM2 are structured similarly and contain similar content. The main difference is that SIM1 uses the 7-bit GSM character set encoding, including extended characters, while SIM2 uses the 16-bit UCS2 type 80 encoding wherever possible. In keeping with the choice of languages supported by the respective character sets, the languages used for SIM1 are English and French and for SIM2 are English and Japanese. Similarly, SIM1 encodes language preferences in LP, and SIM2 uses ELP. Both single segment and long multi-segment concatenated SMS messages are included in the reference data as well as EMS messages containing black and white graphics.

SIM3 contains both 7-bit GSM and 16-bit UCS2 character sets. Some items it includes are the following:

- ADN entry with an alpha-identifier encoded entirely in 7-bit GSM extended characters
- LND entry with a circularly linked EXT1 extension chain

- Concatenated message comprising more than 4 segments
- Two-segment concatenated message with each segment encoded using a different character set
- Message timestamp with an irregular GMT time zone offset.

Several card files are defined: GemExplorer.xml, USIMeraIII.xml, and Standard.xml. The first two card files listed are associated with specific developer SIMs, which can be used to enable ADM access, as well as CHV1 and CHV2 access. They serve as a model for preparing card files for other developer SIMs. The last file listed is for use with common SIMs issued by cellular carriers. The file can be used to supply CHV1 and CHV2 values and gain access, if those settings are enabled.

11. Forensic Tool Assessments

In 2005 and 2007 NIST conducted in depth studies on the capabilities and limitations of an extensive range of mobile forensic tools, including forensic SIM tools [Aye05, Aye07]. Assessments were performed using exemplar devices manually populated with reference data. The results for forensic SIM tools indicated a number of inaccuracies in different tools, including the following ones:

- Information could not be acquired from certain SIMs through the supported interface
- The remaining number of CHV attempts was not provided
- Data was rendered inconsistently in displays and reports
- Recovered data entries were truncated when displayed
- Recovered numeric data and English characters were not always decoded or translated correctly
- European and Asian character sets used in phonebook and message entries were not properly decoded
- Certain EMS messages were completely missed or their content unable to be recognized and rendered correctly
- New versions of a tool occasionally failed to perform as well as a previous one.

Through practice and use of the tools, forensic examiners could devise ways to work around many of the problems. For example, if an error exists for a data item at a high level of abstraction, such as translated data, a lower layer of abstraction that renders the data correctly could be used instead to compensate. Nevertheless, it was troubling that many of the errors existed at all and an indication of a narrow scope of testing being carried out by the tool manufacturers.

While some tool manufacturers worked diligently to correct identified problems, others did not. One contributing factor may be that written descriptions of subtle problems can be difficult to interpret and reproduce. Having a SIM containing data identified as a source of trouble for a tool greatly simplifies communication and provided the motivation to develop an application and reference set of test data described in this report. The application, called SIMfill, and reference test data are available for downloading from NIST.[3]

11.1 Current Assessment

In 2009, SIMfill was used to assess a number of popular forensic SIM tools. The forensic products are used by a large number of examiners. Results are not presented for each tool, nor are the tools identified in this report. Instead, the results are discussed collectively to illustrate the types of inaccuracies that might be encountered in general. The reason for this is twofold.

---

[3] The distribution can be found at
http://csrc.nist.gov/groups/SNS/mobile_security/mobile_forensics_software.html.

First, approximately half of the tool manufacturers have indicated that identified problems would be corrected in the next version. Therefore, some or all of the problems may already be fixed at this time. Second, the assessment process is relatively simple to perform using SIMfill and the basic reference data. It is better to experience firsthand assessment of a preferred SIM tool, than to rely on a secondhand assessment.

Examples of the results discussed in this report are illustrative of the results obtained in our assessment. The examples address the highest level of abstraction provided by a tool. For illustration, the examples involve data condensed from one or more actual test cases. The test cases from which the assessment examples were derived do not require a developer SIM and can be carried out on a 2G SIM or backwards compatible 2G/3G USIM, with disabled CHV1 and CHV2 settings or by providing those values via the card file.

11.2 ADN Example

As mentioned earlier, phonebook data contained in the ADN EF is commonly sought after information. Figure 4, discussed previously, provides an example. Two separate test conditions apply. The first involves the alpha identifier for the name or tag associated with the number; the second involves the number entry, which overflows into EXT1. The 7-bit GSM alphabet is used for the identifier in this example, with paired septets used to represent the left and right bracket. Each row of Table 3 contains a result obtained from one or more forensic tools assessed and a comment on any associated inaccuracy.

Table 3: Tool Results for ADN Example

Name	Number	Other	Comments
John <home>	30130197597580008000 9999		Left and right brackets in name represented instead by less than and greater than signs.
John <home>	30130197597580008000 9999	List of EXT1 Records: 2	Same as above. Output also lists all EXT1 entries containing overflow data.
John [home]	30130197597580008000 9999		Correct.
John [home]	30130197597580008000		No indication is given that any overflow data exists in EXT1.
John [home]	30130197597580008000	Link to First EXT1 Entry: 2	Correct. Output indicates where additional EXT1 overflow data can be found.
John [home]	+854513FFFFFFB01A301301 9759758000		The number is prepended with other data. No indication is given that any overflow data exists in EXT1.

The third and fifth rows both show correct results, but handled in different ways. With the former, along with the name, the forensic tool assembles the full number for display. With the latter, along with the name, the tool displays only the portion of the number contained in the ADN entry. However, a link is provided that indicates where additional portions of the number can be found in EXT1.

22

The first and second rows show the special extended characters of the left and right braces being decoded inaccurately by the forensic tools. Interestingly, the success or failure of a tool to process extended characters in ADN entries seems to be relatively independent of the outcome the tool might have when processing those characters in other EFs, such as the SPN or SMS EFs. Finally, the fourth and sixth rows show a failure by a forensic tool to indicate that additional overflow numbers exist in EXT1. With the latter, other data is also incorrectly prepended.

Note that a problem exists with some forensic tools, if the EXT1 data entries form a circular list (e.g., an entry pointing back to itself). Two of the tools assessed entered an infinite execution loop when processing this condition and failed to terminate successfully. The problem manifests itself in those tools that attempt to assemble the full number field from the overflow entries and fail to check for a loop condition. It illustrates an area where defensive measures could be taken to handle data that is purposefully poisoned.

11.3 SMS Example

Similar to ADN, SMS entries, including entries flagged as deleted, contain commonly sought after information. Figure 6, showing a 3-segment concatenated message, forms the basis of this example. In this instance, however, the message is deleted and only the last segment remains intact, not overwritten by other segments. The message body is encoded using the UCS2 character set. Table 4 contains the results obtained from the various forensic tools and includes comments on any associated inaccuracies.

Table 4: Tool Results for SMS Deleted Segment Example

Reference Number	Body	Segment Index	Segment Count	Comments
66	{and the last.	3	3	Correct.
	{and the last.			No segment or reference numbers provided, making it difficult to deduce whether this segment comprises the entire message.
66	äand the last.	3	3	Miscellaneous character substituted for the left brace.
	{.a.n.d. .t.h.e. .l.a.s.t...	3	3	UCS2 encoded English characters improperly decoded and rendered.

For a deleted concatenated message, the segment index and segment count numbers are needed to determine what exactly was recovered. Otherwise, the recovery of a single segment of a multi-segment deleted message could give an examiner the false impression that the recovered segment is the complete message. The first and second rows illustrate contrasting perspectives, in which the latter omits the needed data provided by the former. The third and fourth rows illustrate a different problem involving the decoding and rendering of UCS2 encoded information. The former cannot handle a certain special character, while the latter seemingly treats each 8-bit portion of the 16-bit encoding independently.

EMS objects appearing in an SMS segment add complexity to the decoding process. The reference data contains only simple graphic objects used in picture messages such as "I ♡ you."

Most tools are able to recognize and render these graphic objects correctly. Some tools are only able to recognize the objects, but not render them. A few tools cannot recognize the objects and interpret them as data, which produces unpredictable results. While EMS is not widely in use, present day handsets are capable of creating EMS content and the defining standard is still active. Various kinds of EMS content could be used as an anti-forensic mechanism to raise doubt in the capabilities of those forensic SIM tools unable to recognize and process them.

11.4 LAI Example

Data recovered from the LAI are relied on occasionally to determine the location area code for the network carrier last contacted before the phone was turned off. Figure 12 gives the details for the levels of abstraction involved in this example for determining the network carrier. The left side shows the generic transformations that occur, while the right side shows the specific data involved in the example. The 310 country code is for the U.S. and the 26 network code for T-Mobile. For North America, the MNC can be 2 characters long, unlike many other regions of the world, such as Europe. In addition, networks can merge, be acquired, or simply rebranded, which may affect the carrier's identifier.

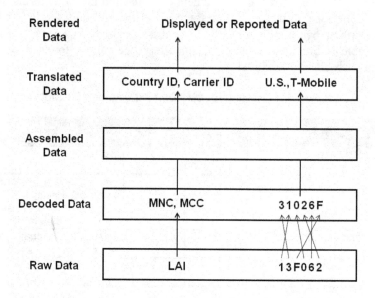

Figure 12: LAI Example—Levels of Abstraction

For the LAI example, a forensic tool may present the data from any of the 3 content layers shown in Figure 12 (i.e., data assembly is not involved). The decoded and translated forms of data are often presented together, because of the possibility of ambiguities in translation. The raw data may also be available as an option. Table 5 shows the results obtained from the various forensic tools and includes comments on any associated inaccuracies.

Table 5: Tool Results for LAI Example

Decoded Data		Translated Data		Comments
MCC	MNC	MCC	MNC	
31026				Decoded MCC and MNC not individually identified.
31026		United States		Decoded MCC and MNC not individually identified. Only MCC able to be translated.
31026		United States	Unknown	Same as above, except that MNC explicitly reported as an unknown value.
		United States	Western Wireless Voicestream	Translated MNC indicates a former network carrier.
310	26	United States of America	T-Mobile USA	Correct.

The first through third rows illustrate correctly decoded data, but the MCC and MNC parts are not identified individually. The second and third rows also exemplify the correctly translated MCC and an inability to translate the MNC. The fourth row illustrates the MNC translated to a former network carrier whose network was acquired by T-Mobile. The fifth row shows the MCC and MNC correctly translated.

The results from past and recent work indicate that assessments of mobile forensic tools can reveal subtle inaccuracies that exist. While the approach discussed in this report is suited for identity modules, it is not immediately clear whether the same or a similar approach could be used to populate handsets and how that might be realized. Figure 13 shows one possibility. The adaption is to use agent applications that are platform dependent, coded in a suitable language, and executed directly on the handset. Many platform families allow middleware development and support a common Application Programming Interface (API) suitable for this purpose. The application and data could be brought to the handset through various means, such as a memory card or data transfer, and the same means used to retrieve the summary report.

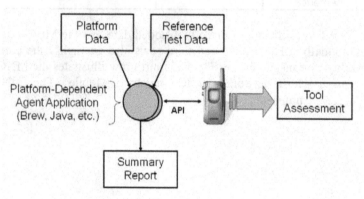

Figure 13: Agent Application Data Flow

The platform data and reference test data would be coded in XML as before. The platform data would identify characteristics of the handset needed by the agent application to populate it. Ideally, that information would allow the application to run on a wider range of systems and perform correctly. The reference test data would be the same for all handsets. That is, the reference data would be comprehensive, but used selectively by the agent application, based on the platform data and the characteristics of the platform encoded into the agent.

Handset data is much more wide-ranging than data on identity modules and presents several challenges. The first is that some reference data items cannot be encoded conveniently in XML. One way to cope with this issue is to use the XML reference data specification to describe those parts of the entry that are amenable to the encoding and to provide a link to the more complex encoded content type. This technique is used in the current set of reference data for identity modules to represent and populate EMS graphic content.

The second challenge is determining whether the API available is sufficient to populate all data items of interest. It may be that for some platforms the API is limited in some respect and an augmented means of data population is required. For example, it would be reasonable to expect the middleware API to support the creation of a submitted multimedia message, but perhaps not a delivered multimedia message. For this situation, a more-basic native API might be required or even a second network-based application to simulate a message server. Further work is required to determine the practicability of the adapted approach outlined for handsets.

13. Summary

This report presents a methodology for populating mobile devices to create reference materials suitable for use in assessing the recovery capabilities of forensic tools.   The methodology involves a data driven application and companion reference data tailored to the device being target. Identity modules are used to explain the technique in detail for a specific type of device and to highlight the associated benefits.

The assertion is that with such a technique, more comprehensive test cases involving a broader range of character sets, data structures, and EFs can be prepared far more easily than could be done through other means, manual or automated, and provide a more rigorous basis for validation. An application and reference data set for populating SIMs were produced to support this contention and demonstrate the concept and principles involved. They have been made publicly available for others to experiment with and to modify to suit specific needs.

This report also discusses potential ways of adapting the technique used for identity modules for possible application to handsets. While some limitations exist, in principle, it could prove viable. Further work is needed to determine whether the adaption outlined or a similar extension of the approach is suitable in practice.

14. References

[3GPP07]   Specification of the Subscriber Identity Module - Mobile Equipment (SIM - ME) interface, 3rd Generation Partnership Project, TS 11.11 V8.14.0 (Release 1999), Technical Specification, June 2007, <URL: http://www.3gpp.org/ftp/Specs/archive/11_series/11.11/1111-8e0.zip>.

[3GPP08]   Technical Specification Group Core Network and Terminals - Alphabets and language-specific information, 3rd Generation Partnership Project, TS 23.038 V9.0.0 (Release 9), Technical Specification, September 2009, <URL: http://www.3gpp.org/ftp/Specs/archive/23_series/23.038/23038-900.zip >.

[3GPP09a]   Technical Specification Group Core Network and Terminals - Technical realization of the Short Message Service (SMS), 3rd Generation Partnership Project, TS 23.040 V9.0.0 (Release 9), Technical Specification, June 2009, <URL: http://www.3gpp.org/ftp/Specs/archive/23_series/23.040/23040-900.zip>.

[3GPP09b]   Technical Specification Group Core Network and Terminals - Numbering, addressing and identification, 3rd Generation Partnership Project, TS 23.003 V8.5.0 (Release 8), Technical Specification, June 2009, <URL: http://www.3gpp.org/ftp/Specs/archive/23_series/23.003/23003-850.zip>.

[3GPP09c]   Technical Specification Group Core Network and Terminals - SIM/USIM internal and external interworking aspects, 3rd Generation Partnership Project, TR 31.900 V8.0.0 (Release 8), Technical Specification, February 2009, <URL: http://www.3gpp.org/ftp/Specs/archive/31_series/31.900/31900-800.zip>.

[Aye05]   Rick Ayers, Wayne Jansen, Nicolas Cilleros, Ronan Daniellou, Cell Phone Forensic Tools: An Overview and Analysis, NISTIR 7250, October 2005, <URL: http://csrc.nist.gov/publications/nistir/nistir-7250.pdf>.

[Aye07]   Rick Ayers, Wayne Jansen, Ludovic Moenner, Aurelien Delaitre, Cell Phone Forensic Tools: An Overview and Analysis Update, NISTIR 7387, March 2007, <URL: http://csrc.nist.gov/publications/nistir/nistir-7387.pdf>.

[Dea05]   Tony Dearsley, Mobile Phone Forensics – Asking the Right Questions, New Law Journal, July 29, 2005, pp. 1164-1165.

[Eps01]   David M. Epstein, Kevin L. Lothridge, William J. Tilstone, The Use of Certified Reference Materials in Forensic QA, 13th INTERPOL Forensic Science Symposium, Lyon, France, October 16-19, 2001, http://www.interpol.com/public/Forensic/IFSS/meeting13/Discussion/Discussion2.pdf

[Goo03]   Amanda Goode, Forensic Extraction of Electronic Evidence from GSM Mobile Phones, IEE Seminar on Secure GSM & Beyond, Digest No. 2003/10059, February 11, 2003.

[ITU06]   The International Telecommunication Charge Card, International Telecommunications Union, Telecommunication Standardization Sector (ITU-T), Recommendation E.118, May 2006, <URL: http://www.itu.int/rec/dologin_pub.asp?lang=e&id=T-REC-E.118-200605-I!!PDF-E&type=items>.

[Jan06]   Wayne Jansen, Rick Ayers, Forensic Software Tools for Cell Phone Subscriber Identity Modules, Conference on Digital Forensics, Association of Digital Forensics, Security, and Law (ADFSL), April 2006, <URL: http://csrc.nist.gov/groups/SNS/mobile_security/documents/mobile_forensics/JDFSL-proceedings2006-fin.pdf>.

[Jur06]   Leon Juranić, Using Fuzzing to Detect Security Vulnerabilities, INFIGO-TD-01-04-2006, Infigo Information Security, April 25, 2006, <URL: http://www.infigo.hr/files/INFIGO-TD-2006-04-01-Fuzzing-eng.pdf>.

[SWG09]   SWGDE Recommendations for Validation Testing, Version 1.1, Scientific Working Group on Digital Evidence, January 2009, <URL: http://www.swgde.org/documents/swgde2009/SWGDE%20Validation%20Guidelines%2001-09.pdf >.

[Wil03]   Svein Willassen, Forensics and the GSM Mobile Telephone System, International Journal of Digital Evidence, Volume 2, Issue 1, Spring 2003, <URL: http://www.utica.edu/academic/institutes/ecii/publications/articles/A0658858-BFF6-C537-7CF86A78D6DE746D.pdf>.

www.ingramcontent.com/pod-product-compliance
Lightning Source LLC
Chambersburg PA
CBHW082106070326
40689CB00054B/4719